Freight Train Running
A Biography of Buck Owens

By Linda Stacey
Illustrated by Angela Gia

Graphic Design by Karlene Copenhaver

Bakersfield City School District Educational Foundation
Bear State Books

ISBN 978-1-892622-27-3

Library of Congress number

How to order additional copies:

Bakersfield City School District Foundation
Buck Owens Book Project
1300 Baker St.
Bakersfield, CA 93305
661-631-4600

www.bcsd.com

Price is $14.95 (includes CA sales tax) plus $5.00 shipping within the U.S.

Libraries should contact the BCSD Educational Foundation for a price quote for quantities.

Copyright 2006 by the BCSD Educational Foundation

Published by Bear State Books
P.O. Box 96
Exeter, CA 93221

Acknowledgements

This book project would not have originated without the vision and encouragement of the
Bakersfield City School District Foundation Board directors and support staff:
Board Directors: Kenton Weir, Jr. (President), Philip Field (Vice President), Dr. Jean Fuller, Superintendent (Secretary/ex officio),
Edward Herrera, Dayna Nichols, Dee Slade, Wayne Stapley, Brian Mendiburu, Vincent Rojas,
Rudy Barrera, Pam Giumarra, Dick Taylor, Renee Wylie, and Raymond Chaffee.
Support Staff: Debor Farrell, Mike Stone, Sarah Futrell Baron, Debbie Verdugo, Carol Reichert, Sandra Yoon, and Susan Rice.

The ongoing support from Buck Owens and Jim Shaw saw the project to fruition.

Additional support came from Kathy Walker and Steve Gabbitas.

Thanks to Ramona and Gilbert Gia for researching the background photos.

Accolades go to Linda Stacey, Angie Gia, and Karlene Copenhaver for their creative spirits
that blended text, pencil drawings, and graphic design to provide a feast for the eyes and a lasting memory for the brain.

Thanks to Chris Brewer as a guiding light in the publishing process.

And many, many thanks to the people who proofed, commented, and read the manuscript through its various changes.

All proceeds from the sale of this book will fund educational projects for BCSD students.

Sandra Yoon, Coordinator,
Library Media Services

Bakersfield City School District 2006

This book is dedicated to the students in the Bakersfield City School District.

A call went out over Bakersfield's KUZZ country radio station one hot summer day. Buck Owens was performing *Streets of Bakersfield* under the huge BAKERSFIELD sign outside of the Crystal Palace. His fans were invited to come and sing along.

Country Music Television was filming the event as part of a special, *Top Ten Country City Songs*. Buck's local fans came out, despite the heat, to sing their hearts out.

One family defined them all. The grandparents had two-stepped to the *Orange Blossom Playboys* at the *Blackboard*. The parents enjoyed *Hee Haw* as kids. Everyone danced to *Buck Owens and the Buckaroos* on weekends at the Crystal Palace. They were proud to support Buck Owens.

Buck was born Alvis Edgar Owens, Jr., on August 12, 1929. His parents, Maicie and Alvis, Sr., were sharecroppers on a cotton farm outside of Sherman, Texas, just south of the Red River.

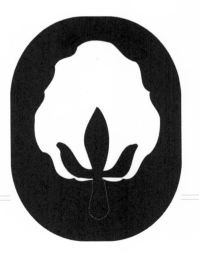

He was the second of four children. Mary was the oldest, then came little Alvis, Melvin, and Dorothy.

They had a mule named Buck. One day, when he was about three or four, he marched into the house and announced that he was named Buck, too!

The name stuck.

Times were tough in the 1930's. The Owens family headed west in 1937 to build a better future. They got as far as Phoenix, Arizona when their trailer hitch broke. They had family in nearby Mesa and settled there.

Buck's dad found work to do at the dairy and fruit farms in Arizona.

Sometimes, they traveled to the fertile San Joaquin Valley in California to harvest vegetables, peaches, potatoes, and cotton.

Despite this back-breaking work, the family was very poor. Buck knew what it was like to go to bed hungry. He wore holes in the bottoms of his shoes. He had hand-me-down clothes. His mother, not the barber, cut everybody's hair.

Buck dreamed of a better life. A fire began to burn in him. He didn't know how, but he would be somebody…someday.

18

School became part of the answer. To follow the farm work, Buck had to change schools a lot. He hated book reports and homework, but if he sang songs or performed in school plays, he could improve his grades.

Music had always been a part of his family life. His mother, Maicie, played piano and taught him gospel songs. They listened to the Grand Ole Opry on the battery-operated radio.

One night, as Buck lay stretched out listening on the living room floor, the dream began to take shape. "I will sing on that stage someday! I swear!" he declared.

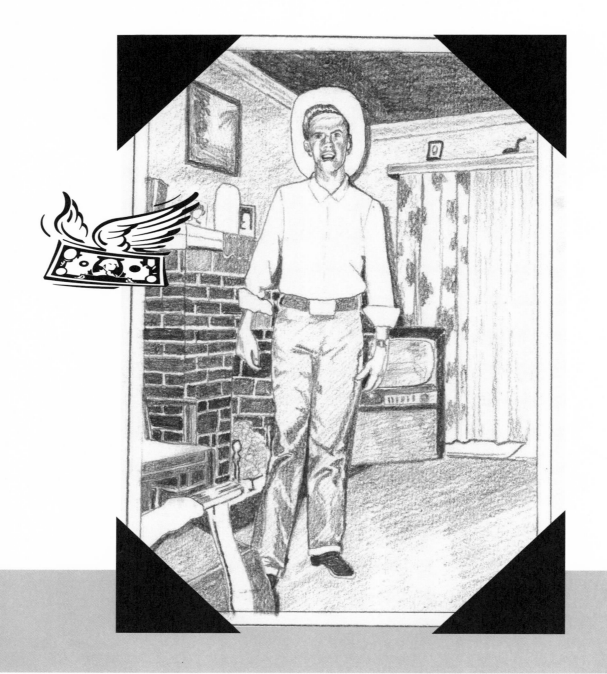

At 13, Buck had finished 8th grade. He worked all summer doing "a man's work for a man's pay." He stood six feet tall! He saved his money and started high school. A few months later, the money he had earned was gone. He begged his parents to let him quit school and go back to work because his money was needed to help support the family. These were different times.

With so many men off to war in 1942, there was plenty to do for a big guy like Buck. He worked for Western Union, loaded fruit trucks, and polished cars. In the evenings, he listened to his dad play harmonica while his uncles played guitar. They listened to the megawatt radio "X" stations from Mexico. Music became his love.

At Christmas, Buck's parents gave him a mandolin and later, a Regal guitar. He quickly learned a few chords from his mother, then taught himself to play.

By 1951, Buck moved to Bakersfield, California. The oil industry and farm work was familiar, but most of all, the country music scene was taking hold.

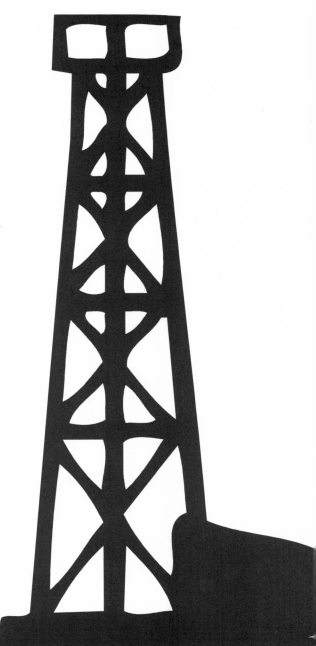

Buck joined *Bill Woods & the Orange Blossom Playboys,* the house band at the famous *Blackboard.* It was the top country music nightclub. Buck became the lead singer and guitarist.

Buck switched to a Fender Telecaster guitar. With this, he added an edgy introduction to *You Better Not Do That* by Tommy Collins. This unique sound would help change Buck's musical future.

Tommy Collins took Buck with him on tour. In 1954, they played at The Grand Ole Opry. Buck's childhood dream had come true.

Buck and Don Rich made the honky tonk circuit across the United States. *Buck Owens and the Buckaroos* headed to the top of the charts with *Kicking Our Hearts Around* and *You're For Me.*

Act Naturally was Buck's break-away hit, staying at number one for a month. His distinctive style was unmistakable. *Love's Gonna Live Here, My Heart Skips a Beat,* and *Together Again* dominated the charts in 1963 and 1964.

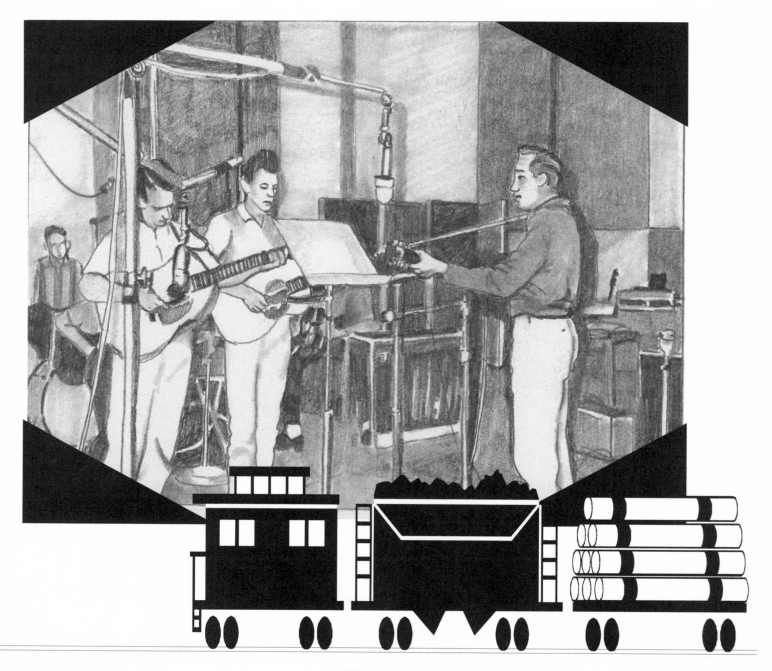

42

Buck Owens had found his unique style in that upbeat 2/4 rhythm. He wanted a freight train sound that would sound "like a locomotive comin' right through the front room." *I Don't Care* and *Tiger By the Tail* came through like a freight train to radios everywhere.

Buck continued to play on the road. *Crying Time* and *Streets of Laredo* were hits. Buck made a pledge in the *Music City News,* " I shall sing no song that is not a country song.... Country music and country music fans made me what I am today, and I shall not forget it."

Buck Owens and the Buckaroos played to a sold out *Carnegie Hall* in New York City in 1966. The band proudly put on their best performance and recorded it live.

Television opportunities came in the 60's. *Hee Haw, with Buck Owens and the Buckaroos,* became the top country music show. With Roy Clark, he brought country music stars, laughter, and patriotism to living rooms across America.

Buck Owens performed on a red, white, and blue acoustical guitar. With his endorsement, Chicago Musical Instruments and Sears marketed a similar guitar, selling to thousands of aspiring country music fans and musicians.

Buck Owens inspired younger musicians like Dwight Yoakum, who credited Buck Owens and his original sound for his own success. They performed Buck's hit, *Streets of Bakersfield,* and toured together.

The producers of the *Bammy Awards* wanted Buck and Ringo Starr to perform a duet of their hit, *Act Naturally*. Even better, they recorded it.

Country Music Hall of Fame!

1996

Buck Owens was inducted into the Country Music Hall of Fame in 1996. He had made the big time.

58

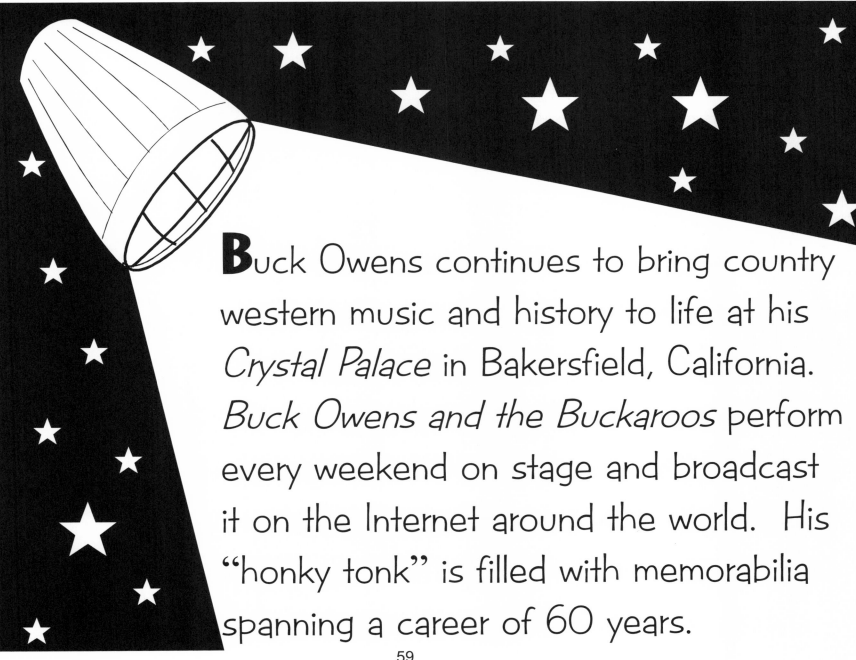

Buck Owens continues to bring country western music and history to life at his *Crystal Palace* in Bakersfield, California. *Buck Owens and the Buckaroos* perform every weekend on stage and broadcast it on the Internet around the world. His "honky tonk" is filled with memorabilia spanning a career of 60 years.

BUCK OWENS

Buck has had a life of hardship and pain, but one of success and fame, too. Most of all, he has found the life he wanted, in music.